WiND

IS A

DANCE

Written by Debra Kempf Shumaker

Illustrated by Josée Bisaillon

Kids Can Press

You can feel wind ... but you can't see it.
What *is* wind?

Wind is a dance — a dance of air.
Warm air leaps high, while cool air bows low.

Day by day, fast or slow, wind changes.

Some days ...

Wind is a butterfly —
fluffing flower petals
and ruffling riverbank grasses.

A breeze is a light-to-moderate wind. Leaves rustle, branches quiver. A light breeze is a perfect wind for blowing bubbles. A stronger breeze is a good wind for flying kites.

Sometimes, wind is a supportive teammate —
helping, nudging,
encouraging you from behind.

A tailwind blows on your back, helping you move forward.

But if you switch directions ...

Wind is an ornery opponent —
blocking, stopping,
determined to slow you down.

A **headwind** pushes against you. If it's really strong, a headwind can make it hard to move! Tailwinds and headwinds are actually the same wind. They have different names based on the direction you are facing.

Other days, wind is an excited puppy —
barging in, fast and strong,
swinging its tail,
tipping and toppling things to the ground.

A gale is a moderate-to-strong wind. On water, waves
become high and foamy. On land, leaves toss and turn.
Branches and trees sway. Twigs and limbs may break.
It's best to stay inside during these strong winds!

As the dance of air moves faster, wind blows stronger.
Brisker, colder ...

wind is a boxer —
jabbing, snapping,
throwing snow until everything is buried in white.

A **blizzard** is a snowstorm with very strong winds. A blizzard blows snow so hard that it is difficult to see, and can be dangerous outside. But from inside your warm home, it's fun to watch the snow whip around. After the blizzard is done, get out to play!

Swifter, stronger ...

wind is a train —
rumbling straight down the track.
Breaking branches,
tumbling trees,
until finally,
it runs
out
of
steam.

Derecho is Spanish for "straight ahead." As a name for a storm, derecho means a very fast, long windstorm that follows a band of quick-moving thunderstorms in a straight line. If a derecho is coming, get inside! When it's done, you might have to help clean up branches and step around fallen trees.

Even faster ...

wind is a whisk —
churning and whipping
a batter of clouds and rain
over the warm ocean.
Growing, swelling,
shoving, pushing,
building waves that tumble
and crash ashore.

A hurricane is a large, spinning storm that starts with very fast winds over warm ocean water. Since the high winds can raise tides and push water ashore, hurricanes can be very destructive if they make landfall. If a hurricane is approaching your area, you might have to help board up windows and evacuate. If your family doesn't evacuate, stay inside in a windowless interior room or storm shelter when the storm comes.

Fastest, frantic!

Wind is a top —
stretching down from the clouds
to the ground,
twisting, turning, tearing up
everything in its winding path.

A **tornado** is a rapidly spinning column of air that comes down from a puffy cumulus cloud — usually a thunderstorm cloud — and touches the ground. The pressure inside the tornado is lower than outside of it, so the tornado acts like a vacuum and sucks up anything in its path. If a tornado warning is issued where you live, immediately get into a storm shelter, a basement or an interior windowless room, like a bathroom or closet. Tornados are very dangerous and can destroy buildings.

As all dances end, so do windstorms.

They may stop suddenly —
like a dancer landing after a leap.
Or they may slowly fade away ...
like a ballerina's fluttery tiptoe
off the stage.

And on some days, wind hardly blows at all.
Then, wind is a feather —
barely tickling your skin as it brushes on by.

Yes, wind is a dance of air —
shifting, changing
hour by hour,
day by day.

How would you describe the wind today?

More about Wind

As the sun warms the Earth, the air around the Earth warms, too. But because the Earth is spherical and rotates on a tilted axis as it revolves around the sun, the air warms unevenly. Warm air is less dense than cold air, so the warm air will rise, and cold air moves in to take its place. This movement of air is wind.

Scientists define different winds by how fast they move and what direction they move in.

Here is more information about the types of wind mentioned in this book (listed in order of appearance):

breeze: a light-to-moderate wind. Wind speed ranges from 6 to 49 km (4 to 31 mi.) per hour.

tailwind: a wind that blows in the same direction you are moving

headwind: a wind that blows in the opposite direction you are moving

gale: a moderate-to-strong wind. Wind speed ranges from 50 to 88 km (32 to 54 mi.) per hour.

blizzard: a snowstorm with very strong winds. In Canada, a storm is considered a blizzard when winds reach or exceed 40 km (25 mi.) per hour and blow for at least four hours. But in the United States, a storm is a blizzard when winds reach or exceed 56 km (35 mi.) per hour and last at least three hours. Blizzards blow snow so hard that it is difficult to see anything beyond 400 meters or a quarter of a mile — that's three city blocks! In North America, blizzards happen most often in northern areas but can occur almost anywhere it gets cold enough to snow.

derecho: a severe windstorm that follows a band of fast-moving thunderstorms. For wind to be classified as a derecho, the path of the windstorm must be over 400 km (249 mi.) long with wind speeds of at least 93 km (58 mi.) per hour. They happen most often in the American Midwest on warm, muggy evenings in late spring and early summer but can occur in other parts of North America and the world any time of year.

hurricane: a storm that develops over warm ocean water near the equator. As the warm air rises, it leaves low air pressure, which funnels in moisture from the ocean. This creates thunderstorms, which in turn pull in more warm air. The storms start to spin. If this wide, rotating mass of air has wind speeds of at least 119 km (74 mi.) per hour, it is classified as a hurricane. As a hurricane nears land, its winds push water toward the shoreline and raise the water level above the tide, which can cause major flooding and destruction. Hurricanes typically happen in summer or early fall in the Atlantic Ocean and Caribbean Sea.

tornado: a rapidly spinning column of air centered around low air pressure that comes down from a base of clouds during a thunderstorm. Wind speeds range from 105 km (65 mi.) per hour to over 322 km (200 mi.) per hour! Tornados happen most often during spring and summer east of the Rocky Mountains, though they can form anywhere at any time of year.

Measuring Wind

The Beaufort Scale was created by Sir Francis Beaufort in 1805 to help sailors describe wind. At first, it was used for wind on the sea, but land descriptions were added later.

Beaufort Number	Wind Speed per hour	Description	Sea Conditions	Land Conditions
0	<1 km <1 mi.	Calm	Flat	Calm
1	1–5 km 1–3 mi.	Light air	Ripples without crest	Wind motion visible in smoke
2	6–11 km 4–7 mi.	Light breeze	Small wavelets	Leaves rustle
3	12–19 km 8–12 mi.	Gentle breeze	Large wavelets	Smaller twigs in constant motion
4	20–28 km 13–18 mi.	Moderate breeze	Small waves	Small branches begin to move
5	29–38 km 19–24 mi.	Fresh breeze	Moderate longer waves	Smaller trees sway
6	39–49 km 25–31 mi.	Strong breeze	Large waves form with foam crests	Large branches in motion
7	50–61 km 32–38 mi.	Near gale	Sea heaps up and foam begins to streak	Whole trees in motion
8	62–74 km 39–46 mi.	Gale	Moderately high waves with breaking crests	Twigs broken from trees
9	75–88 km 47–54 mi.	Severe gale	High waves with dense foam	Light structural damage
10	89–102 km 55–63 mi.	Storm	Very high waves. The sea surface is white.	Trees uprooted. Significant structural damage.
11	103–117 km 64–72 mi.	Violent storm	Exceptionally high waves	Widespread structural damage
12	118+ km 73+ mi.	Hurricane	Sea completely white with driving spray	Massive and widespread damage to structures

An instrument called an *anemometer* measures wind speed. Simple anemometers have three or four cups connected to a horizontal arm on a vertical pole. When the wind blows, the cups rotate, which causes the rod to spin. The harder the wind blows, the faster it spins. Wind speed is calculated by the number of rotations, or spins, in a certain amount of time. Since winds can speed up or slow down quickly, the speed is averaged over a short period of time. Now, most weather stations use digital anemometers, which use fan blades rather than cups.

The top three wind gusts measured on land by an anemometer, according to wunderground.com, are:

- 407 km (253 mi.) per hour at Barrow Island, Australia on April 10, 1996
- 372 km (231 mi.) per hour on Mount Washington, New Hampshire, USA on April 12, 1934
- 341 km (212 mi.) per hour at Paso Real de San Diego, Cuba on August 30, 2008

Learn how to make your own anemometer at www.weatherwizkids.com.

Sources

Books:

Challoner, Jack. *Hurricane & Tornado*. New York, NY: DK Children, 2021.

Cosgrove, Brian. *DK Eyewitness Books: Weather*. New York, NY: DK Children, 2022.

Williams, Jack. *Pocket Guide to the Weather of North America*. Washington, D.C.: National Geographic Partners, 2017.

Websites:

www.noaa.gov
www.weather.gc.ca
www.weather.gov
www.weatherwizkids.com

To Jack, who loves weather even more than me.
To Tom, the wind beneath my wings. — D.K.S.

ACKNOWLEDGMENTS

Many thanks to Amanda Kis, PhD, at the University of Oklahoma School of Meteorology, for her insight and expertise on the text of this book.

Published in Canada and the U.S. by Kids Can Press Ltd.
25 Dockside Drive, Toronto, ON M5A 0B5

Kids Can Press is a Corus Entertainment Inc. company

www.kidscanpress.com

The artwork in this book was rendered in mixed media.
The text is set in Avenir.

Edited by Kathleen Keenan
Designed by Andrew Dupuis

Printed and bound in Buji, Shenzhen, China, in 3/2024 by WKT Company

CM 24 0 9 8 7 6 5 4 3 2 1

LIBRARY AND ARCHIVES CANADA CATALOGUING IN PUBLICATION

Title: Wind is a dance / written by Debra Kempf Shumaker ; illustrated by Josée Bisaillon.

Names: Shumaker, Debra Kempf, author. | Bisaillon, Josée, author.

Description: Includes bibliographical references.

Identifiers: Canadiana (print) 20230585604 | Canadiana (ebook) 20230585612 | ISBN 9781525308758 (hardcover) | ISBN 9781525311635 (EPUB)
Subjects: LCSH: Winds — Juvenile literature. | LCSH: Metaphor — Juvenile literature. | LCSH: Figures of speech — Juvenile literature. | LCGFT: Picture books. | LCGFT: Instructional and educational works.

Classification: LCC QC931.4 .K46 2024 | DDC j551.51/8 — dc23

Kids Can Press gratefully acknowledges that the land on which our office is located is the traditional territory of many nations, including the Mississaugas of the Credit, the Anishnabeg, the Chippewa, the Haudenosaunee and the Wendat peoples, and is now home to many diverse First Nations, Inuit and Métis peoples.

We thank the Government of Ontario, through Ontario Creates and the Ontario Arts Council; the Canada Council for the Arts; and the Government of Canada for their financial support of our publishing activity.